AM-PFS

I0439680

Comptroller of the Currency
Administrator of National Banks

Personal Fiduciary Services

Comptroller's Handbook

August 2002

AM

Asset Managemen

As of May 17, 2012, this guidance applies to federal savings associations in addition to national banks.*

Personal Fiduciary Services   Table of Contents

Overview

Examination Procedures

Appendices

References

Personal Fiduciary Services   Overview

This booklet provides an overview of personal fiduciary services, their associated risks, and a framework for managing those risks. It applies to personal accounts administered by a national bank in a fiduciary capacity as defined by 12 CFR Part 9, Fiduciary Activities of National Banks.

This booklet also provides national bank examiners with expanded examination procedures for these activities that supplement the minimum core assessment standards in the "Large Bank Supervision" and "Community Bank Supervision" booklets of the *Comptroller's Handbook*. This booklet's examination procedures, which are optional, may be used when specific products or risks warrant review beyond the core assessment.

Background

Personal fiduciary services are part of a growing and competitive market frequently referred to as "private wealth management," "private client services," or "private banking." However these services are described, they usually entail providing a broad range of financial services to affluent persons, their families, and their businesses. At the core of these services are fiduciary relationships and investment management.

Section 92a(a) of the National Bank Act authorizes the OCC to permit national banks to act in eight enumerated fiduciary capacities (trustee, executor, administrator, registrar of stocks and bonds, guardian of estates, assignee, receiver, committee of estates of lunatics). If a state permits state banks, trust companies, or other corporations that compete with national banks to act in capacities in addition to the enumerated ones, section 92a(a) empowers the OCC to authorize national banks to act in those capacities.

12 CFR Part 9 sets forth the standards that apply to the fiduciary activities of national banks. This part applies to all national banks and federal branches of foreign banks that act in a fiduciary

capacity. For the purposes of 12 CFR Part 9, fiduciary capacity is defined as the following:

- Trustee, executor, administrator, registrar of stocks and bonds, transfer agent, guardian, assignee, receiver, or custodian under a uniform gifts to minors act;

- Investment adviser, if the bank receives a fee for its investment advice;

- Any capacity in which the bank possesses investment discretion on behalf of another; or

- Any other similar capacity that the OCC authorizes pursuant to 12 USC 92a.

This regulation is generally permissive and authorizes specific fiduciary activities for national banks unless those activities are restricted or prohibited by applicable law. Applicable law for a national bank is defined in 12 CFR Part 9.2(b) as:

- The terms of the instrument governing a fiduciary relationship;

- The law of a state or other jurisdiction governing a national bank's fiduciary relationships;

- Applicable federal law governing those relationships (for example, federal securities laws); or

- Any court order pertaining to the relationship.

While Part 9 reflects common fiduciary principles and its provisions are not specific to a particular state law or a type of fiduciary instrument, certain parts are linked to other fiduciary laws. For example, the fiduciary compensation provision at 12 CFR Part 9.15 authorizes a national bank to charge a "reasonable fee" for its services unless compensation terms are set or governed by other applicable law. Certain provisions of Part 9 are restrictive and prohibit certain fiduciary activities unless applicable law expressly authorizes those activities. For example, the conflicts of interest provision at 12 CFR Part 9.12 prohibits a bank from engaging in self-dealing or entering into conflict situations unless authorized by applicable law.

A fiduciary relationship involves a duty on the part of the fiduciary to act for the benefit of the other party to the relationship concerning the matters within the scope of the relationship. Fiduciary law is designed to protect the party who gives fiduciary power (grantor) to another party (fiduciary) and those who may ultimately benefit from that transfer of power (the beneficiaries) from the significant risks inherent in the fiduciary relationship. The underlying premise of fiduciary law is to afford grantors legal protections that might otherwise be unavailable, too costly, or impractical to obtain.

The enforcement of fiduciary law, however, is neither a guarantee against loss nor an assurance of expected performance by the fiduciary. Courts have recognized that even sound fiduciary administration and investment practices can produce unexpected losses.

Fiduciary Accounts

National banks provide fiduciary services to a variety of personal account types. These services were once provided primarily for the very wealthy, but are now offered to a broader range of clients. Personal fiduciary accounts can be divided into three major groups:

- Court-supervised accounts,
- Trust agreements, and
- Investment accounts.

Court-Supervised Accounts

Estates, guardianships, and certain trusts are administered under the jurisdiction of an appropriate court of law. The court's role is to protect the interests of the deceased, minors, and incompetents. The court of jurisdiction formally appoints the fiduciary in accordance with law and reviews and approves all subsequent acts of the fiduciary related to that particular account. In some states, testamentary trusts may also be administered under the order and protection of a court.

Estates

Planning. An estate is the property left by a person who dies. That person is usually referred to as the "decedent" or if he or she had a will the "testator." Estate planning addresses the use, conservation, and disposition of an estate. It is the process by which persons plan for the transfer of their property during their lives and for its disposition on their deaths. A comprehensive estate plan allows a person to:

- Dispose of assets according personal wishes,
- Establish effective tax strategies,
- Provide for self and family in the event of incapacity,
- Obtain professional asset management,
- Select personal representatives,
- Name guardians for minor children,
- Maintain privacy of personal information, and
- Provide protection for the beneficiaries of the estate.

The development and implementation of an effective estate plan require different types of legal and financial expertise as well as good communication among members of the estate planning team. Wills, trust agreements, powers of attorney, living wills, letters of instruction, and beneficiary designations established through insurance policies and retirement plans are common documents in estate planning.

An important part of creating an estate plan is the selection of suitable individuals or corporations to serve in the various fiduciary capacities. These capacities include the executor or personal representative, trustee, guardian for minor children, and an agent or attorney-in-fact to serve under a durable power of attorney. A power of attorney is an instrument authorizing a person to act as an agent or attorney-in-fact for another person. The person given the power will be able to make financial and legal decisions on behalf of the person granting the power. A durable power of attorney remains effective even if the grantor becomes incapacitated.

Generally, state law permits only a bank or a trust company to serve as a corporate fiduciary. A corporate fiduciary is generally not allowed to serve as a guardian of the person or as an agent under a power of attorney for health care. A corporate fiduciary may serve as a guardian of the estate and, in some circumstances, as an agent under a power of attorney for financial or property purposes.

A bank fiduciary's role in the estate planning process is one of facilitator, and extreme care should be taken in working with clients and advisors. It is the role of the client's attorney to create the estate plan and draft the legal documents. Although a bank fiduciary may discuss legal concepts and estate planning alternatives with clients and prospects, only an attorney should actually draw up the estate plan.

Administration and Settlement. Probate is one of the ways to pass ownership of estate property to a decedent's survivors. This is the legal process by which a court validates a decedent's will and supervises the administration of the estate. The probate estate is the portion of the estate that must go through the probate process before it can be transferred. Certain estate interests, such as living trusts, life insurance policy proceeds not payable to the estate, payable upon death accounts, and property held jointly with rights of survivorship are generally not included in the probate estate.

Probating an estate requires the appointment of a personal representative to administer the estate. The representative may be called the executor, administrator, or personal representative of the estate if appointed as such in a decedent's will. If a decedent does not have a valid will (dies intestate), or does not name a personal representative in his or her will, the court will appoint someone to administer the estate, also called an administrator. The court will issue "letters testamentary" or "letters of administration" granting the personal representative authority to administer the estate.

The appropriate court determines the validity of a decedent's will. Once the court validates the will, it appoints the personal representative. Upon formal acceptance of the appointment, the personal representative will administer the estate in accordance with the terms of the will and other appropriate orders. In some situations, state law will override the terms of a valid will. For example, a decedent who attempts to "cut a spouse out of his or her will" may be prevented from so doing by state laws that provide the surviving spouse with a right to a certain percentage of the estate.

In most states, a will is valid only when written, signed, and witnessed in accordance with specific statutory requirements. Generally, the testator must be competent, of legal age, and not under duress. A will may be deemed invalid by a court if it fails to meet statutory guidelines.

Until it receives authority from the probate court, the personal representative has no power to dispose of any part of the estate, except to pay reasonable funeral expenses or to take such action as it deems necessary to preserve estate property. Pending formal authorization by the court, the personal representative may take appropriate action to handle family issues and protect estate property. Such actions might include the following:

- Locate, read, and interpret the will and any codicils thereto;
- Meet with family members and counsel to discuss immediate concerns and problems;
- Make funeral, burial, and perpetual care arrangements as directed, or as circumstances require;
- Take immediate steps for the temporary protection of estate property pending probate of the will;
- Locate financial records and determine nature and location of estate property;
- Determine if there are outstanding lawsuits initiated by or against the decedent;
- Change locks to secure real property;
- Change address to forward mail to the representative;
- Check property insurance coverage and increase if prudent;

- Notify financial institutions and certain creditors of death, including closing any revolving credit accounts; and
- Notify the social security administration, and any pension plan making payments, of the decedent's death.

After the personal representative receives court authorization, it may begin formal settlement of the estate. The duties of a personal representative are governed by the provisions of the decedent's validated estate documents, state probate codes, court orders, and sound fiduciary principles. Important administrative responsibilities include the following:

- Identify, possess, safeguard, appraise, and invest estate assets. This includes determining if the estate has outstanding claims against third parties. Insurance coverage should also be reviewed and adjusted where needed.

- Prepare and file inventory with the court, if required by state law or the court.

- Notify heirs and beneficiaries. Most states require that a formal notice be sent to the appropriate heirs and beneficiaries of the decedent.

- Notify interested parties and creditors. This notice formally advises parties with claims against the estate to present them within the time frame reflected in the notice. The representative also contests any improper claims against the estate.

- Prepare federal, state and local income tax returns; prepare applicable federal and state estate or inheritance tax returns, and pay tax liabilities. The representative has the power to sell estate assets in order to pay liabilities and expenses of the estate.

- Pay legacies (gifts of personal property), devises (gifts of real property), and bequests, and obtain proper receipts and releases, including estate tax release from the IRS, if appropriate.

- Fund trusts established under will and distribute remaining assets to beneficiaries, including distribution to any pre-existing trusts.

- Submit a final accounting to the probate court and close probate administration. In some states, ongoing accountings may be required by the court.

When the representative files an accounting in court, it is settled judicially and in the formal manner prescribed by law. The accounting is a report of the representative's administration of the estate and provides all parties concerned, including beneficiaries and any unpaid creditors, with the opportunity to comment on what has or has not been done. The court then customarily approves the final accounting and discharges the representative, unless objections are filed and sustained.

Guardianships

A guardianship (for purposes of this booklet, the term "guardian" shall include conservators) is a court-appointed fiduciary relationship established to protect a person who is not of legal age or who is mentally or physically incapacitated. This person is commonly referred to as a "ward." A guardian is an individual or trust institution appointed by a court to care for and manage the property of the ward. Once the court has determined that a guardian is necessary, it enters an order and issues a letter of guardianship. This document is the guardian's authority to act on behalf of the ward.

In most states, there are two kinds of guardians: a guardian of the person and a guardian of the property or estate. A bank would normally be appointed guardian of the property used to maintain the ward, and a relative or friend of the ward would be appointed guardian of the person.

The fiduciary's role as a guardian is analogous to the role of a court-appointed personal representative or trustee, only it is more restrictive. The guardian's objectives are to meet the needs of the ward and to prudently manage the account's assets. A guardian's basic duties are to:

- **Gather the assets of the ward.** Ownership of the property is legally transferred to the name of the guardian with the ward retaining a beneficial interest in the property.

- **Manage the property in the best interests of the ward.** The guardian is responsible for the property's protection and investment. The guardian's objective should be to make the property productive and to satisfy the living requirements of the ward. Some states restrict the types of investments that may be made by guardians.

- **Make periodic accountings to the court.** Under most state statutes, accountings are required annually.

- **Terminate and distribute the property.** Generally, either of two events terminates the guardianship: the ward's death or resolution of the ward's incapacity. If the ward dies, the guardianship immediately terminates and the assets are distributed to the executor of the ward's estate. If the guardianship is based on the ward's lack of legal age, it terminates when the ward reaches the age of majority. If the guardianship is based on another kind of incapacity, it terminates when the court declares the ward competent.

Personal Trusts

Personal trust services are a significant part of most national banks' fiduciary business. A trust is a flexible legal instrument whereby one person is enabled to deal with property for the benefit of another person. A trust can be used for many purposes such as:

- Estate planning,
- Professional asset management,
- Disability planning,
- Privacy,
- Probate avoidance,
- Providing financial support for the settlor and others, and
- Other special needs and goals.

Trust Law

Trusts are peculiar to the Anglo-American system of law. English common law established the general framework for United States trust law. Trust law in the United States developed through the judicial system rather than through federal or state legislation, although most states have now adopted statutes that are specific to trusts.

The principles of common trust law and their application in judicial proceedings over time have been consolidated and interpreted in two primary publications. These publications are the basic guides to trust law in the United States:

- *Restatement of the Law, Trusts*, Second and Third Editions, American Law Institute.

- *The Law of Trusts, Fourth Edition*, Austin W. Scott.

The National Conference of Commissioners on Uniform State Laws has created and adopted several uniform trust statutes that give states a framework for establishing their trust and probate statutes. A list of these statutes, which only apply if adopted by a state's legislature, is provided in Appendix B. States will often modify the draft statutes to fit their own circumstances.

Upon acceptance of a trusteeship, a national bank must administer the trust in accordance with applicable law. When a trust instrument is silent about an issue, consistent with 12 CFR Part 9.7, the laws of the state in which the bank acts in a fiduciary capacity generally become the applicable law. Most states now have statutes that prescribe the scope of a trustee's powers, duties, responsibilities, and liabilities. Violations of laws and regulations may constitute a breach of trust for which the trustee can be held liable.

Characteristics of a Trust

A trust is a fiduciary relationship in which a person or entity, the holder of the legal title to property, is subject to an equitable obligation to keep or use the property for the benefit of another person or entity. The creator of a trust is known as the settlor, grantor, testator, donor, or maker. To be valid, a trust must demonstrate or meet the following standards:

- An intent to create a trust by a legally competent settlor.
- A present act of declaration or transfer by the settlor.
- The existence of trust property.
- Designation of a trustee.
- Identification of beneficiaries.
- Delivery of trust property to the trustee.

The settlor can create a trust during his or her lifetime under agreement or declaration (living trust) or through the execution of a valid will (testamentary trust). The settlor transfers legal title of the property to the trustee as a fiduciary, while the equitable or beneficial interest in the property (income and principal) is assigned to persons designated by name or class as beneficiary.

A trust agreement (or instrument) is the formal written document that sets forth the terms of the trust. The trust agreement is generally prepared or reviewed by an attorney. A trust agreement can be established by will, by an instrument other than a will, or by order of a court. The trust agreement will normally:

- Define the settlor's intent;
- Appoint a trustee;
- Identify the beneficiaries;
- Define what the beneficiaries are to receive; and
- Define the powers, duties, and compensation of the trustee.

Trust Property and Accounting. The property of a trust is referred to as its "corpus." The corpus is composed of principal (invested assets) and income (return derived from the principal). Trust accounting is based on the separation of income from principal.

Depending on the terms of the trust agreement, principal and income are used and distributed in varying ways. In addition, the receipt of or disbursement from income and principal affects the value of trust corpus and its eventual distribution to beneficiaries as directed by the terms of the trust agreement.

Trust accounting is the activity of recording and accounting for transactions within the trust account. Transactions are the activities that affect the principal and income positions of a trust account. Transactions occur when

- Assets are bought and sold,
- Deposits are made,
- Income is collected,
- Disbursements occur,
- Cash moves in and out,
- Corporate actions occur, and
- Fees are paid and collected.

Cash received from transactions is categorized as income or principal depending upon its source. The trust agreement may contain specific guidance for the application of principal and income transactions. If the trust agreement does not provide adequate guidance, state law provides guidance. Many states have adopted the Uniform Principal and Income Act of 1997 as recommended for enactment by the National Conference of Commissioners on Uniform State Laws. States that have not adopted the uniform act have enacted versions of it. Trust administrators must be familiar with their state's statutory guidelines.

Trust Beneficiaries. Beneficiaries are the parties who will receive the equitable benefits of a trust. The party or parties entitled to income from the trust are called income or present-interest beneficiaries. The parties entitled to receive the trust principal, or "corpus," are called principal beneficiaries or remaindermen.

Income beneficiaries can be described as either (1) mandatory, meaning that under the terms of the trust income must be paid out to them regularly, or (2) discretionary, leaving to the trustee whether to pay out or not pay out some or all of the trust income in any period. Sometimes income and/or principal is to be paid to some or all of a group of beneficiaries, in amounts and at times determined by the trustee in its discretion. This is referred to as the power to "spray" or "sprinkle." Income not paid out is usually added to trust principal and reinvested.

The discretionary power to spray or sprinkle is usually left to the trustee, but this power can be governed by language in the trust. For example, a trust might give the trustee discretion to pay out trust income "in such amounts and at such times, or not at all, and for any reason, to the exclusion of one or more persons if there is more than one in the class, as my trustees shall determine in their absolute discretion." An example of a "class" would be the children of the settlor. Alternatively, the trust instrument can make the discretionary power subject to an objective standard such as "as my trustees shall determine necessary and appropriate for the support and maintenance of the income beneficiary."

Some income beneficiaries also receive the power to withdraw trust principal from time to time or upon specified events. This power, however, can have adverse income and transfer tax results to the beneficiary and should be carefully considered by trust planners.

There are two types of principal beneficiaries: remaindermen and principal invasion beneficiaries. Remaindermen are the person or persons who receive the trust principal remaining when the trust terminates. A principal invasion beneficiary, who is usually an income beneficiary, can be given portions of the trust principal, usually at the discretion of the trustee during the trust term.

Like the discretionary power to spray or sprinkle income, the power to invade principal may be without qualification or may be subject to some standard. An unqualified power permits the trustee to give a beneficiary any part or the entire principal at any time, as the trustee determines to be in the beneficiary's best interest, with or without consideration of the beneficiary's personal resources. Alternatively, the trust instrument may permit the trustee to invade principal only in accordance with a specific, ascertainable standard, such as for the beneficiary's support and maintenance, medical and health needs, or education. Some trusts allow beneficiaries to request payments from principal.

Powers of Appointment. A trust may grant a power of appointment, usually to the income beneficiary. This power permits its recipient to designate who will receive the trust remainder, perhaps overriding the terms of the trust. There are two classes of powers of appointment: general and special, or nongeneral. A general power gives the holder of the power the right to give the trust property to anyone in the world, including the holder's creditors, the holder's estate, the creditors of the holder's estate, and even directly to the holder.

The Internal Revenue Service considers the holder of a general power of appointment as the owner of the trust property for income and estate tax purposes. For trust law purposes, however, a general power of appointment is not title to property. It only gives the holder the power to designate the ultimate owners of the property. Trust property ownership is deemed to pass from the settlor, not from the holder of the general power of appointment. This holder is considered to be only a conduit between the settlor and the remaindermen.

A special power of appointment is limited in scope, may not be exercised in favor of the holder of the power, and is not the equivalent to ownership for tax or other purposes. An example of language conferring a special power to convey property would be "to such of my children and grandchildren as the donee of the power shall designate."

A power of appointment is exercisable by the holder of the power either during the term of the trust (a lifetime power), upon the trust's termination (a testamentary power), or sometimes at both times. If a donee of a power of appointment fails to exercise it in whole or in part, the trust terms that govern disposal of the trust corpus will control.

Spendthrift Clauses. Trust instruments commonly contain spendthrift clauses. Spendthrift clauses are designed to prevent the payment of funds or disbursement of assets to anyone other than the trust's beneficiary and to prevent creditors of the beneficiary from reaching the trust's assets. They may also be used in a spendthrift trust to restrict what a beneficiary may do with his or her interest in the trust. For example, a spendthrift provision might be used to prevent a beneficiary from assigning or transferring his or her future interest in a trust in order to gain present economic value. This would prevent a beneficiary who has not yet attained the age specified in a trust for receiving trust income or assets from pledging future trust benefits in exchange for current acquisitions or consumption (e.g., a car). It could also prevent a beneficiary who has poor money management skills from selling his interest in a trust meant to provide him with steady income and then squandering the money.

Rule Against Perpetuities. The rule against perpetuities (RAP), which derives from common law, voids any estate or interest that will not take effect or vest within a period established by applicable state law. One notable exception to the RAP is a charitable trust, which may extend into perpetuity. In order to comply with traditional state RAP laws, many governing instruments will contain a RAP savings clause requiring the trust to terminate prior to the completion of lives in being plus 21 years, or prior to other RAP time frames established by the state law governing that particular trust.

Although the RAP remains in effect in most states, there are several jurisdictions that have repealed some or all of RAP. Under the laws of these states, individuals may be able to establish "Dynasty Trusts" that will likely continue for many generations without any state law requirements that they vest within a certain time period.

Types of Trusts

The two most common types of trusts are testamentary and living, or inter vivos, trusts.

Testamentary Trusts. A testamentary trust is established by a testator's will and takes effect only after passing successfully through the probate process following the testator's death. Before the testator dies, a testamentary trust can be modified or revoked by changing the will. The trust is not funded until the death of the testator. After the testator dies, a testamentary trust is irrevocable — that is, it may not be changed or revoked, except by court order.

Since a bank is not a party to the creation of the will, a testamentary trust creates no fiduciary obligations for the bank until the will has been probated and the bank accepts the appointment as trustee. Once a trust department accepts the trust, the trust's terms are binding and help to determine the fiduciary's responsibilities.

Living or Inter Vivos Trusts. A living trust is created under a trust agreement made effective during the settlor's lifetime and is used to manage the settlor's property during his or her life. A living trust may be revocable or irrevocable.

In a revocable living trust, the settlor places his or her property in trust with a trustee, but retains the power to freely withdraw income and principal and change or terminate the trust agreement. The trustee is called upon to act for the benefit of the settlor in the event of incapacity. Upon the settlor's death, the trust becomes irrevocable and to that extent substitutes for a will as to the property it holds. Assets owned in the trust will be distributed at the death of the settlor in accordance with the trust agreement and will not be subject to probate administration.

The tax code treats a revocable trust as not involving a transfer of property, since the settlor retains all interest in it. There is, therefore, no gift tax when legal title to the property is transferred to the trust, and all income and capital gains are taxed to the settlor. A revocable trust is fully taxable upon the settlor's death as part of the settlor's taxable estate. However, this type of trust can be drafted to enable an executor to take certain actions after the settlor's death in order to take advantage of benefits under the tax laws in effect at the time of the settlor's death.

For example, a husband and wife may each establish revocable trusts and upon the death of the first spouse, the trust's assets are directly transferred into one or more credit shelter trusts (see appendix A for definition). This arrangement is used to avoid having monies flow, upon the death of one spouse, directly to the surviving spouse and enables the couple to maximize the benefits of both of their individual estate tax exclusions.

A revocable living trust has other benefits:

- The trustee may provide professional investment management services.

- The trustee collects income from securities and other investments, manages cash, and distributes income in the manner requested by the settlor or outlined in the governing instrument.

- The trust alleviates the settlor's concern about his or her possible incapacity, because a trustee will step in to handle the settlor's affairs.

- The trust avoids a potentially time-consuming, expensive, and public probate process and protects the privacy of the settlor as well as that of his or her beneficiaries.

An irrevocable living trust represents an unalterable transfer of the settlor's property and creates rights for designated beneficiaries, who may include the settlor. Since an irrevocable trust involves a permanent transfer to the beneficiaries, the settlor must pay gift tax on the transfer of property to the trust. Income paid out of the trust is taxed to the beneficiary who receives it. Income not paid out and accumulated by the trust, including realized capital gains, is taxed to the trust.

An irrevocable living trust is generally not included in the settlor's taxable estate, assuming the settlor did not retain an interest in the trust, or a power to change its beneficial interests. Since the trust property was subject to gift tax when the trust was created, no estate tax should be due when the settlor dies. If, however, the settlor has set up a grantor trust, the trust may be included in the settlor's taxable estate, and the trustee may be responsible for paying the tax, depending on the tax apportionment clause in the settlor's will.

The trust instrument will normally state whether a trust is revocable or irrevocable. If the governing instrument is silent, state law will determine the presumption. Irrevocable trusts are extremely difficult to terminate until the purpose of the trust has been fulfilled.

For more information about personal trusts, including several types of grantor trusts, as well as marital deduction trusts, credit shelter trusts, generation-skipping trusts, minor exclusion trusts, charitable trusts, and pre-need funeral trusts, see appendix A.

Powers and Duties of a Trustee

Trustee Powers. A trustee may exercise any power conferred to it by the terms of the trust agreement or applicable statutes without authorization by a court of equity. The exercise of a power granted to a trustee is subject to the fiduciary duties of a trustee described in the next section.

The trust agreement will generally describe the powers given to the trustee and whether such powers are restricted or denied. If the trust instrument is silent concerning a certain power, the trustee should look to applicable statutes regarding the power. Generally, a statutory power granted to a trustee is effective unless the governing instrument of the trust expressly forbids its exercise.

If neither the trust instrument nor applicable law expressly gives a particular power to the trustee, such power may be implied from the general terms and purposes of the trust or from express powers granted by the trust agreement or statute. A trustee should call upon a court of equity to infer such power or seek the consent of beneficiaries prior to exercising the power.

A settlor may choose to give the trustee discretion in exercising a particular power because of the flexibility such an arrangement provides. Discretionary power may be absolute or limited.

A trustee may directly exercise the powers granted to it, or it may delegate authority to an agent or co-trustee under the following circumstances:

- The trust agreement specifically authorizes delegation of the power;
- Applicable statutes authorize delegation of the power; or
- The trustee has received the consent of the beneficiaries or a court order authorizing such delegation.

Trustee Duties. All trustees are subject to a variety of common law fiduciary duties as well as applicable state fiduciary statutes. A national bank is responsible for fulfilling these duties when it formally accepts the trustee appointment. Generally recognized duties of a trustee are:

- *Duty of loyalty.* A trustee must administer a trust solely in the interests of the beneficiaries. This is the most fundamental duty of a trustee. A trustee must not engage in any act of self-dealing.

- *Duty of administration.* The trustee must administer the trust in accordance with its terms, purposes, and the interests of the beneficiaries. A trustee must act prudently in the administration of a trust and exercise reasonable care, skill, and caution. A trustee must only incur reasonable costs of administration.

- *Duty to control and protect trust property.* The trustee must take reasonable steps to take control of and protect the trust property.

- *Duty to keep property separate and maintain adequate records.* A trustee must keep trust property separate from the trustee's property and keep and render clear and accurate records with respect to the administration of the trust.

- *Duty of impartiality.* If a trust has two or more beneficiaries, the trustee must act impartially in investing, managing, and distributing the trust property, giving due regard to the beneficiaries' respective interests.

- *Duty to enforce and defend claims.* A trustee must take reasonable steps to enforce claims of the trust and to defend claims against the trust.

- *Duty to inform and report.* A trust must keep qualified trust beneficiaries reasonably informed about the administration of the trust and of the material facts necessary for them to protect their interests. Some jurisdictions also impose a duty to provide an accounting to qualified beneficiaries.

- *Duty of prudent investment.* A trustee who invests and manages trust property has a duty to comply with the prudent investor rule unless otherwise stated by the terms of the trust or provided by state law. This duty is tied to the duty to use reasonable care and skill to make the trust property productive.

If a trustee has special skills or expertise, or is named trustee in reliance upon the trustee's representation that the trustee has special skills or expertise, the trustee must use those special skills or expertise while administering the trust.

If a trust requires special skills or expertise that a trustee does not possess, the trustee may delegate certain duties and powers to a third-party agent if the power to delegate is authorized by applicable law. The trustee must comply with applicable law when delegating a duty or power to a third-party agent. Applicable law generally requires the trustee to use reasonable care, skill, and caution in:

- Selecting an agent;

- Establishing the scope and terms of the delegation, consistent with the purposes and terms of the trust; and

- Periodically reviewing the agent's actions in order to monitor the agent's performance and compliance with the terms of the delegation.

Investment Accounts

National banks are significant providers of fiduciary investment services for personal clients. A bank may provide discretionary investment management services or it may only provide investment advice for a fee with limited or no investment discretion. Investment accounts for which the bank has investment discretion or provides investment advice for a fee are defined as fiduciary accounts by the OCC in 12 CFR Part 9, Fiduciary Activities of National Banks, and are subject to the regulation.

In a discretionary investment account, the bank is given the sole or shared authority to purchase and sell assets and execute transactions for the benefit of the principal, in addition to providing investment advice. The bank's investment authority is usually subject to investment policy guidelines established in the investment account contract. The bank does not receive legal title to the assets placed in the investment account as it would if the bank served as trustee for a trust.

In an investment advisory account, the bank may provide portfolio management and advisory services for a fee. These services may include investment analysis and advice, trade processing, performance measurement, and securities safekeeping and custody.

The "Investment Management Services" booklet of the *Comptroller's Handbook* provides additional supervisory guidance for investment accounts.

Risks

The provision of personal fiduciary services creates risk to a bank that must be identified, measured, controlled and monitored. The types and level of risk are potentially unlimited because each personal account is a separate legal relationship that involves unique client characteristics and fiduciary duties and responsibilities.

The following sections address risk from the perspective of the OCC's risk assessment system. In most cases, the risk factors that will apply to personal fiduciary services are transaction, compliance, reputation, and strategic risks. Definitions for each factor are in the "Large Bank Supervision" and "Community Bank Supervision" booklets of the *Comptroller's Handbook*.

Transaction Risk

Transaction risk is inherent in the provision and administration of personal fiduciary services. When serving as a fiduciary, a bank will normally be responsible for processing and reporting many types of transactions and a large part of its revenue may come from transactions. The business is by its nature transaction intensive, and a fiduciary's success will depend on how well it gathers, processes, and reports transactions and information. Examples of transactions, accountings, and information reports are:

- The acceptance and establishment of accounts;
- The receipt and disbursement of account income;
- The purchase, sale, valuation, and performance measurement of account investments;
- The review and execution of discretionary account distributions;
- The maintenance of account financial records and the preparation and distribution of client statements;
- The preparation and submission of account tax returns and related reports; and
- The preparation of internal financial records and information reports.

The recordkeeping, accounting, and reporting systems necessary to operate a profitable personal fiduciary business can be complex and expensive to acquire and maintain. A bank must have fiduciary information systems and internal controls that are appropriate to the types and levels of risk inherent in each of the personal fiduciary services provided by the bank. It is also important that a bank have an adequate and well-trained staff.

Account losses that result from a bank's failure to properly safeguard assets or process transactions can lead to violations of applicable law, client litigation, and loss of business. Financial losses can be large in relation to a bank's earnings and capital. A damaged reputation from poor management of transaction risk can significantly harm a bank's ability to compete and be financially successful in the personal fiduciary business.

Compliance Risk

A bank that does not comply with applicable law can suffer lawsuits, regulatory supervisory action, and severe damage to its reputation. The financial impact of litigation, regulatory action, and criminal activity is difficult to estimate, but it can be significant in relation to earnings and capital. In addition, such adverse situations may be highly publicized in the bank's market area and could further damage a bank's reputation.

A bank fiduciary must comply with the terms of the governing document (assuming such terms are legal) that establishes the fiduciary relationship. Trust agreements, wills, agency agreements, and court orders establish legal relationships that set forth the duties and obligations of the fiduciary. These are legally enforceable documents and failing to comply with them can result in financial losses.

A bank fiduciary must comply with a multitude of federal, state, and local laws and regulations to which the bank and each individual account are subject. These include, but are not limited to, trust investment law, securities law, banking law, tax law, contract law, environmental law, consumer protection law, and criminal law. Corporate fiduciaries have long been held to the highest standard of care by the court systems.

Bank personnel must also comply with applicable bank policies and internal operating procedures and control systems. Personal fiduciary account administration can be complex and requires sound legal expertise, an ethical and highly trained staff, and an effective internal control system. Failing to comply with internal policies and procedures can lead to poor risk selection, strategic business failure, wasted financial resources, client lawsuits, and increased regulatory oversight.

Strategic Risk

The personal fiduciary services business can be an important component of bank profitability and shareholder value. Financial success requires a sound strategic planning process embraced by the board and senior management. The business requires a substantial provision of financial, human, and technological resources. Expenditures for personnel, information systems, product development and distribution channels, and internal control systems must be appropriate for the diversity and complexity of an organization's fiduciary operations. Inadequate strategic planning and business plan implementation can lead to poor earnings performance, wasted capital, and diminished shareholder value.

Reputation Risk

Success in providing personal fiduciary services depends on the quality of the bank's reputation with its current and prospective clients and the general marketplace. Because a high degree of trust is implicit in any fiduciary relationship, a sound reputation is essential to attract and retain personal fiduciary accounts. Personal clients are demanding in terms of expected investment performance, product selection, information reporting, service, and the use of advanced technology. Competition for personal clients is very strong, and negative publicity, whether deserved or not, can damage a bank's ability to compete. In particular, disputes with account beneficiaries can increase reputation risk.

A bank's reputation in the marketplace depends on its ability to effectively manage transaction, compliance, and strategic risks, as well as the financial risks of each personal fiduciary account. Litigation, regulatory action, criminal activity, inadequate products and services, below-average investment performance, poor service quality, and weak strategic initiatives and planning can lead to a diminished reputation and, consequently, to an inability to compete and be successful.

Risk Management

This section describes how national banks should manage risk associated with personal fiduciary services. Risk management must effectively assess, control, and monitor risk associated with these activities. Because risk strategies and organizational structures vary, there is no single risk management system that works for every bank. Each bank should establish a risk management system suited to its own needs and circumstances. The "Asset Management" booklet of the *Comptroller's Handbook* provides additional guidance on risk management systems.

Board and Management Supervision

Personal fiduciary services must be managed by or under the direction of a bank's board of directors. A board may assign fiduciary management authority to any director, officer, employee, or committee of the bank and may use the qualified personnel and facilities of its affiliates to fulfill its fiduciary responsibilities (See 12 CFR Part 9.4).

The board may also purchase services related to the exercise of fiduciary powers from a third-party vendor. If the board uses the services of a third-party vendor, it must ensure that the activity is conducted in a safe and sound manner and in compliance with applicable law. The board and senior management must provide proper oversight of those given the authority to administer personal fiduciary services, including a third-party vendor. OCC Bulletin 2001-47, "Third-Party Relationships," provides additional risk management guidance for these types of service arrangements.

The board and senior management are responsible for ensuring that the fiduciary risk management system includes sound internal controls and an adequate and effective audit program. If personal fiduciary services represent a significant fiduciary activity, they must be included in the bank's fiduciary audit program required by 12 CFR Part 9.9.

The "Asset Management" booklet of the *Comptroller's Handbook* contains additional information on the OCC's expectations for board and management supervision of fiduciary activities.

Policies and Procedures

National banks are required by 12 CFR Part 9.5 to adopt and follow written policies and procedures that are adequate to maintain their fiduciary activities in compliance with applicable law. The scope and detail of fiduciary policies and procedures will depend upon the complexity of the services provided. In general, the more complex the fiduciary services offered, the greater the need for formalized and detailed policies and procedures.

12 CFR Part 9.5 also requires a bank's fiduciary policy to address the following items, if appropriate:

- Broker placement practices,
- Use of inside information relating to security transactions,
- Self-dealing and conflicts of interest,
- Selection and retention of legal counsel, and
- Investment of fiduciary funds.

The following topics should also be addressed in the policy:

- Account acceptance,
- Account administration, and
- Management information reporting.

The capacity and duty of committees or individuals authorized to sign agreements on behalf of the bank with clients and other third-parties should be specified in policy. The possibility of lawsuits claiming that a party did not adequately perform its fiduciary responsibilities should motivate banks to describe and document their fiduciary activities and responsibilities as well as to monitor compliance carefully.

Account Acceptance

Pre-Acceptance Reviews

12 CFR Part 9.6(a) requires a national bank to review a prospective account before accepting it. This review must document whether the bank can effectively administer the account. The bank must determine whether it has the expertise and systems to properly manage the account and whether the account meets the bank's risk and profitability standards. A bank is under no moral or legal obligation to accept all business that it is offered.

The early identification of risk will help the bank control the amount of risk it accepts and price risk properly. Bank policy should provide guidance on the types of fiduciary accounts that are desirable and should define specific conditions for accepting new accounts. Procedural controls should be established to ensure compliance with account acceptance policies.

The bank should establish a due diligence process for reviewing each prospective account. The due diligence process should consider applicable risk management issues and ensure compliance with the bank's policies and procedures. The results of an account's due diligence review should be documented and recorded in the appropriate bank record file.

The assets used to fund the account should be reviewed as part of the pre-acceptance review. The committee should not accept an account that holds assets that are beyond the skill and expertise of the bank's staff to properly administer. The bank would be expected to acquire the appropriate expertise before accepting the account or to decline the appointment. Assets that are more likely to be illiquid, such as real estate, family businesses, oil and gas properties, foreign assets, and art, should be carefully reviewed.

Conflicts Of Interest

Before accepting a fiduciary account, the bank should review the governing instrument for potential conflicts of interest. A conflict of interest normally arises when the bank's ability to act exclusively in the best interest of the client is impaired. If such a conflict exists, the bank should take appropriate action to resolve the conflict before accepting the account. Refer to the "Conflicts of Interest" booklet of the *Comptroller's Handbook* for additional information.

Successor Trusteeships

Under common law, a trust will not fail for lack of a trustee. Generally, four conditions may result in a trustee vacancy:

- Disclaimer (i.e., refusal to act) by a person or corporation appointed to act as a trustee.
- Dissolution of a corporate trustee or the death of an individual trustee.
- Resignation of a trustee in accordance with the terms and conditions of the trust instrument.
- Removal of a trustee in accordance with the terms and conditions of the trust instrument.

If a trustee vacancy occurs, a successor trustee will be appointed in accordance with (1) the terms and conditions of the trust instrument, (2) procedures set forth in applicable state statutes, or (3) a court having equity jurisdiction over the trust. Generally, a successor trustee may exercise all of the powers granted to the original trustee, unless the trust instrument provides to the contrary.

A national bank may be asked or appointed by a court to act as a successor trustee. Serving in this capacity may subject the bank to potential liability stemming from the acts of the prior trustee. Under common law, a successor trustee may be liable if it retains an improper investment made by the predecessor trustee but does not attempt to marshal the fiduciary property (that is, to inventory and appraise it) or compel the predecessor to redress a breach of trust.

It is the duty of the successor trustee to enforce any claim that the account may have against the predecessor trustee.

Before accepting a successor trusteeship, a bank should perform a due diligence review of all prior account activity, identify and review all account assets, and, if possible, obtain indemnification from the predecessor for any actions taken prior to the assumption of the fiduciary relationship. Some states have passed statutes that afford protection to the successor trustee from acts of the predecessor. However, a bank should have a written record indicating that a proper due diligence investigation has been performed or have appropriate releases from the court or all beneficiaries. A court order, or releases from all life tenants, remainder interests, and contingent beneficiaries, may provide some protection from the assumption of successor trustee liability.

Exculpatory Clauses

A will or trust instrument may include an exculpatory clause that attempts to relieve the trustee from certain liabilities. The trustee is not, however, always protected by such a provision, and it does not protect trustees from a breach of trust or from actions that are illegal. Before accepting a fiduciary account, the bank should obtain legal advice concerning the effectiveness of such clauses in trust documents.

Co-Trustees

The trust instrument may provide for the bank to administer the trust with a co-trustee. The co-trustee may be one or more persons or another bank or trust company. Co-trustees are added to provide special expertise or to ensure that certain family interests are considered when decisions are made regarding the account. Trust instruments generally require co-trustees to act in unison.

When a national bank acts as a co-trustee with another bank, each bank must perform its duties as though it were the sole fiduciary. A co-trustee agreement between two banks must set forth the terms and conditions under which they will jointly carry out their duties and obligations. Because of the potential liability associated with acting as a co-trustee, the trust instrument should be reviewed by each bank's legal counsel and be approved by its board of directors. An indemnity agreement between bank co-trustees is only recommended when one bank is much larger or more skillful than the other bank.

Post-Acceptance Account Review and Establishment

Upon acceptance of a fiduciary account for which the bank has investment discretion, the bank must promptly review all assets of the account to evaluate whether the assets are appropriate for the account, in accordance with12 CFR Part 9.6(b). The appropriateness of each asset will depend on the purpose of the account and the needs and circumstances of account beneficiaries. An investment policy statement should be created that establishes the account's investment objectives and strategies. Refer to the "Investment Management Services" booklet of the Comptroller's Handbook for additional information on investment policy statements.

It is common to review a synoptic record during the initial post-acceptance review. Synoptic information is a summary of the governing instrument that states the bank's powers, any special circumstances (assets that must be retained, proprietary mutual fund language, etc.), as well as information on beneficiaries. The synoptic information should also include a brief summary of the account's investment policy statement.

Account administrators often use checklists to ensure that they obtain all information needed to establish an account. These checklists usually itemize all the documents required to open an account (governing document, asset schedules, fee schedules, court documents, etc.).

The fiduciary relationship is formally established through a written legal document such as a trust agreement or agency contract. The governing document should clearly specify the bank's fiduciary duties and obligations and articulate the nature and limits of each party's status as agent or principal. Provisions in the instrument about co-fiduciaries (co-trustees), whether individuals or other financial institutions, must be analyzed to determine whether the bank has any unusual or special responsibilities.

Once the account has been formally established, it is funded by the deposit of assets. Funding involves current assets of the trust and assets that are subsequently purchased for the account or added by the settlor. The account administrator may provide the operations department an inventory of assets to be deposited into the account so that appropriate accounting entries can be made. It is important that all assets be accurately described in the inventory.

Account Administration

It is the fundamental duty of a fiduciary to administer an account solely in the interest of clients. The duty of loyalty is of paramount importance and underlies the entire administration of personal fiduciary accounts. A successful administration will meet the needs of clients in a safe and productive manner while equitably balancing the interests of each beneficiary.

The governing instrument, such as a will, trust agreement, court order, or agency contract, controls the administration of a fiduciary account. State statutes and provisions of 12 CFR Part 9 control when the governing instrument is silent. A body of common law has developed over time to help determine a fiduciary's responsibilities when neither statute nor the governing instrument address a particular issue.

Recordkeeping and Document Security

In accordance with 12 CFR Part 9.8, Recordkeeping, a national bank must

- Adequately document the establishment and termination of each fiduciary account and maintain adequate records;

- Retain fiduciary account records for a period of three years from the later of the termination of the account or the termination of litigation relating to the account; and

- Ensure that fiduciary account records are separate and distinct from other records of the bank.

The fiduciary is expected to have sound controls over the governing instrument and other original documents. The controls should ensure that original documents that are filed with court authorities are properly authenticated and preserved for future accountings. Copies may be retained in account files, but original documentation should be maintained in a centrally controlled location. Original board and committee minutes, with attachments noting approvals and actions taken, should receive the same level of safeguarding.

Periodic Account Reviews

12 CFR Part 9.6(c) requires the bank to conduct a review at least once during each calendar year of all assets of each fiduciary account for which it has investment discretion. The review must determine whether account assets are appropriate, individually and collectively, for the account. The review should consider the account's investment policy statement, analyze investment performance, and reaffirm or change the investment policy statement, including asset allocation guidelines. If certain assets are no longer appropriate for the account, those assets should be replaced consistent with prudent investment practices. Items to consider include account objectives, the needs of beneficiaries, and income tax consequences.

Fiduciaries may also perform periodic administrative account reviews to determine whether the account is being administered in accordance with the terms and conditions of the governing instrument. Periodic account reviews are generally completed by an administrative officer working with a designated investment manager or advisor, and are normally submitted to and reviewed by an appropriate fiduciary committee.

Discretionary Distributions

A discretionary distribution power gives a trustee the authority to determine the amount and types of distributions and, in some cases, to select the beneficiaries from among a class or several classes of beneficiaries. Making discretionary distributions is a risky and challenging responsibility of a trustee. Exercising this power may mean that one beneficiary, such as the income beneficiary receiving a distribution of principal, receives a benefit, while another, typically the remainderman, does not.

The proper use of a discretionary power requires sound judgment and a clear understanding of the terms of the trust, the settlor's intention, and the best interests of the beneficiaries. A trustee with discretionary distribution power must fully comply with the income payout and principal invasion standards established by the trust agreement. Failure to do so may violate the trustee's duty of impartiality and constitute a breach of trust.

Effective risk management requires a process to ensure that the decision to make a discretionary distribution is based on standards that are fair to both the income and principal beneficiaries. Bank trustees may handle discretionary distributions in various ways, usually dependent upon the size of the department and the types of accounts administered. Bank policy may limit the dollar amount of discretionary distributions that account administrators can make without a higher level approval. Alternatively, all distributions may have to be approved by a designated fiduciary committee. All discretionary distribution decisions should be adequately supported, documented, and approved by an authorized authority.

Client Communication

Customer service is often the difference between success and failure in the personal fiduciary service business. Most fiduciaries will attest to the benefits of good communication with account principals, beneficiaries, and co-fiduciaries. Very often, consumer complaints and threatened litigation are a direct result of inadequate communication of policies, responsibilities, account objectives and strategies, and other client expectations.

The bank fiduciary should have a system to ensure that a bank representative periodically contacts account principals and beneficiaries to determine whether their financial objectives and circumstances have changed. During such communication, the bank representative should review the account's purpose and investment policy and determine whether it is being administered in a prudent manner and solely in the best interest of the client.

Other Compliance Issues

Personal fiduciary services are subject to the Currency and Foreign Transactions Reporting Act, also known as the Bank Secrecy Act (BSA) and its implementing regulation, 31 CFR 103. A bank must establish policies and procedures to ensure that fiduciary activities comply with the BSA and anti-money laundering laws and regulations, including the Uniting and Strengthening America by Providing Appropriate Tools Required to Intercept and Obstruct Terrorism Act of 2001 (USA PATRIOT Act). The "Bank Secrecy Act/Anti-Money Laundering" booklet of the *Comptroller's Handbook* provides a comprehensive overview of the BSA and anti-money laundering issues and related OCC supervisory policies.

Certain fiduciary customers are covered by Title V of the Gramm-Leach-Bliley Act of 1999, which sets forth provisions addressing the obligations of a financial institution with respect to the privacy of consumers' nonpublic personal information, and the OCC's implementing regulation, 12 CFR 40, Privacy of Consumer Financial Information. The bank must ensure that it complies with this regulation's notice and disclosure requirements as they apply to covered fiduciary accounts. Some states also have consumer privacy laws that should be considered.

Consumer protection statutes and regulations may apply to the activities of personal trusts. A national bank is responsible for ensuring that a trust for which it serves as trustee complies with applicable consumer protection laws and regulations. Failure to do so can result in a breach of the bank's fiduciary responsibilities, beneficiary litigation, and financial and reputation damage to the bank. The *Comptroller's Handbook for Consumer Compliance* contains an overview of the consumer protection laws and regulations applicable to personal trusts. Compliance with these laws and regulations is supervised by the OCC through its consumer compliance examination process.

Account Termination

Accounts may be terminated for a variety of reasons. For example, a personal trust may terminate at a specified time or upon the occurrence of a specified event. In most states, a trust's duration is governed by the rule against perpetuities (21 years past the last beneficiary's death, plus 9 months). Some states, however, have recently repealed that rule, giving trusts in those states no legal ending date. When an account must be terminated, the bank fiduciary is responsible for terminating the account, distributing the remaining assets, and preparing and filing required reports. Risk control processes should be just as strong when terminating accounts as when accepting them.

The governing instrument controls the form and manner of asset distribution. If the instrument is silent as to the form of distribution, the fiduciary is responsible for producing a plan of distribution. This plan should be approved internally and submitted to the beneficiaries. It should consider factors such as

- The type and value of assets,
- Difficulties in dividing the assets,
- Distributions in cash or in kind,
- Tax consequences,
- Releases,
- Timing of distributions,
- Needs and circumstances of the remaindermen, and
- Judicial and beneficiary accountings.

Applicable law may require judicial filings that generate a release of the fiduciary from its obligations. A judicial accounting is often desirable in certain complex accounts even when not required by law. The accounting will bind all of the remaindermen. Often, and particularly in the case of small, noncomplex trust accounts, a trust account may be closed with receipt and release agreements.

Management Information Systems

The board and management must have adequate information systems to assess, control, and monitor risk from personal fiduciary accounts. The following are some examples of appropriate information systems:

- Financial recordkeeping systems such as an automated accounting system designed for the administration and operation of trust accounts.

- Senior management information reports to monitor risk, compliance with policies, and the financial performance of the business. These include financial, audit, compliance, control self-assessments, and legal reports.

- Administrative reports to keep track of the day-to-day administration requirements for each account. These would include cash management reports, delinquency reports, transaction reports, and other types of tickler reports.

- Investment performance reports such as portfolio reviews and transaction reports.

- Customer statements and presentations to report investment holdings, transactions, and performance.

Efficient and effective risk management requires a fiduciary information system that is timely, accurate, relevant, useful, and appropriate for the size and complexity of the fiduciary organization. Appropriate internal controls and financial and human resources must be provided to maintain and protect the bank's information systems.

Personal Fiduciary Services Examination Procedures

Expanded procedures provide detailed guidance on how to examine specific activities or products that warrant supervisory review beyond the appropriate core assessment, which examiners complete using separate standards for large banks and community banks. The use of the following expanded procedures is optional. Examiners decide whether to use them after reaching core assessment conclusions and during pre-examination planning. The decision to use expanded procedures is coordinated with the asset management examiner responsible for planning fiduciary examination activities for the applicable bank and must be adequately documented in the work papers.

If the bank provides personal fiduciary services through an entity for which the OCC is not the primary functional regulator, the appropriate supervisory approach should be discussed with the asset management EIC and bank EIC before commencing any type of examination activity for such an entity. The "Large Bank Supervision," "Asset Management," "Investment Management Services," and "Insurance Activities" booklets of the *Comptroller's Handbook* provide OCC supervisory policies relating to functional supervision.

Planning Activities

Objective: To review the quantity of risk and the quality of risk management relating to personal fiduciary services and reconfirm the objectives, scope and work plans for the planned examination activity.

1.   Consult the following sources of information, if applicable, and review the types, risk characteristics, and distribution channels of personal fiduciary services provided by the bank:

      ❑ OCC information databases.

❑ Previous reports of examinations, analyses, related board and management responses, and work papers.

❑ The asset management profile.

❑ OCC correspondence files.

❑ Call reports.

❑ Supervisory reports issued by other functional regulators.

❑ Fiduciary risk monitoring reports from the board, committees, business lines, risk management groups, compliance, legal, and audit functions.

2. Discuss the following with the fiduciary organization's risk managers:

- Significant risk issues and management strategies;
- Significant changes in strategies, products, services, and distribution channels;
- Significant changes in organization, policies, controls, and information systems; and
- External factors that are affecting services.

3. Develop a preliminary risk assessment and discuss it with the asset management EIC and/or the bank EIC for perspective and examination planning coordination. Consider the following:

- Previous examination conclusions and recommendations;
- Internal risk and control assessments;
- Strategic and business plans;
- New products, services, and distribution channels; and
- Changes in organization, policies, procedures, controls, and information systems.

4. Reconfirm and finalize the examination objectives, scope and work plans to be completed during the examination activity.

Decisions concerning the use of expanded procedures should be clearly documented.

5. If applicable, prepare and submit a revised examination planning memorandum for approval by the asset management EIC that includes the following information:

- Examination activity objectives including a description of the types of accounts, services, or processes to be reviewed.

- The types (on-site and quarterly monitoring), schedules, and projected workdays of the examination activity.

- The scope of examination procedures to be completed, including the use of expanded procedures and risk-oriented sampling guidelines. The memorandum should address the amount of testing or direct verification that may be necessary. The scope of examination activity and the selected procedures should be consistent with the risk assessment and focus on the bank's higher risk activities.

- The examiner resources necessary to complete the activities.

- The types of communication planned, such as meetings and final written products.

6. Finalize the examination's work assignments.

7. Discuss the examination plan with appropriate bank personnel and make suitable arrangements for on-site accommodations and additional information requests.

8. If applicable, contact each examination team member and provide necessary details concerning examination assignments and schedules.

The "Examination Planning and Control," "Large Bank Supervision," "Community Bank Supervision," "Asset Management," and "Community Bank Fiduciary Activities Supervision" booklets of the *Comptroller's Handbook* contain additional guidance on and procedures for examination planning activities.

Personal Fiduciary Services   Quantity of Risk

Transaction Risk

Conclusion: **The quantity of transaction risk from personal fiduciary services is (low, moderate, high).**

Objective: To determine the quantity of transaction risk from the bank's delivery and administration of personal fiduciary services.

1.   Obtain and analyze management information reports relating to transaction processing and reporting within the personal fiduciary organization. Consider the following structural factors:

- The volume, type, and complexity of transactions, products, and services offered through the bank;
- The condition, security, capacity, and recoverability of systems;
- The complexity and volume of conversions, integrations, and system changes;
- The development of new markets, products, services, technology, and delivery systems to maintain competitive position and gain strategic advantage; and
- The volume and severity of operational, administrative, and accounting control exceptions and losses from fraud and operating errors.

2.   Analyze and discuss with management how the following strategic assessment factors affect the quantity of transaction risk related to personal fiduciary services:

- The impact of strategic factors, including marketing plans and the development of new markets, products, services, technology, and delivery systems;
- The impact of acquisition and divestiture strategies; and
- The maintenance of an appropriate balance between technology innovation and secure operations.

3. Analyze and discuss with management how the following external assessment factors affect the quantity of transaction risk related to personal fiduciary services:

    - The impact of external factors including economic, industry, competitive, and market conditions; legislative and regulatory changes; and technological advancement;

    - The impact of infrastructure threats on the bank's ability to deliver timely support and service; and

    - The ability of service providers to maintain the level of service that the bank requires.

4. Obtain and review the most recently completed information technology examination activity:

    - Discus the findings and recommendations relating to personal fiduciary services with bank management.

    - Determine whether commitments for corrective action or other recommendations have been adequately addressed by the organization.

5. Obtain and review the most recently completed OCC examination activity of the bank's fiduciary operations:

    - Discuss the findings and recommendations relating to personal fiduciary services with OCC examiners and bank management.

    - Determine whether the organization has followed through on its commitments to take corrective action or to follow other recommendations.

6. Reach a conclusion on the quantity of transaction risk from personal fiduciary services based on the findings of these and other applicable asset management examination activities.

Compliance Risk

Conclusion: The quantity of compliance risk from personal fiduciary services is (low, moderate, high).

Objective: To determine the quantity of compliance risk from the bank's delivery and administration of personal fiduciary services.

1. Obtain and analyze the types and level of policy exceptions, internal control deficiencies, and law violations that have been identified and reported internally. Review information from the following sources:

   ☐ Board and committee minutes and reports.
   ☐ Risk management and compliance division reports.
   ☐ Control self-assessment reports.
   ☐ Internal and external audit reports.
   ☐ Regulatory reports.
   ☐ Other OCC examination programs.

2. Obtain and analyze the types and volume of litigation and consumer complaints related to personal fiduciary accounts.

3. Discuss significant litigation and complaints with bank management. Determine the risk to capital and the appropriateness of corrective action and follow-up processes. If necessary, refer to the "Litigation and Other Legal Matters" booklet of the *Comptroller's Handbook* for additional procedures.

4. Incorporate the findings of the account sampling and testing performed in the "Quality of Risk Management" examination procedures into the assessment of compliance risk. Consider the level of compliance with

   • The governing instrument,
   • State and local law,
   • Court orders,

- Federal law, and
- Bank policies and operating procedures.

5. Reach a conclusion on the quantity of compliance risk from personal fiduciary services based on the findings of these and other related examination activities. Consider the following factors:

    - The nature, complexity, and extent of fiduciary business activities, including new and planned products and services;

    - The volume and significance of noncompliance and nonconformance with policies and procedures, applicable law, and basic fiduciary principles; and

    - The amount and significance of fiduciary-related litigation and customer complaints.

Strategic Risk

Conclusion: Aggregate strategic risk from personal fiduciary services is (low, moderate, high).

Objective: To identify and estimate strategic risk inherent in the bank's delivery and administration of personal fiduciary services.

1. Obtain and analyze the bank's strategic plan for personal fiduciary services. Consider the following strategic factors:

    *   The magnitude of change in established corporate mission, goals, culture, values, or risk tolerance;
    *   The financial objectives as they relate to the short- and long-term goals of the bank;
    *   The market situation, including product, customer demographics, geographic position, and multi-state operations;
    *   Diversification by product, geography, and customer demographics;
    *   Past performance in offering new products and services;
    *   Risk of implementing innovative or unproven products, services, or technologies;
    *   Merger and acquisition plans and opportunities; and
    *   Potential or planned entrance into new businesses, product lines, delivery channels, or implementation of new systems.

2. Discuss with management and reach conclusions about the effect external factors on strategic risk. Consider the following strategic factors:

    *   Economic, industry, and market conditions;
    *   Legislative and regulatory change;
    *   Technological advances; and
    *   Competition.

3. Obtain and analyze conclusions from the personal fiduciary services "Quality of Risk Management" examination procedures. Incorporate those conclusions into the evaluation

of strategic risk from personal fiduciary services. Consider the following strategic factors:

- The expertise of senior management and the effectiveness of the board of directors;
- The priority and compatibility of personnel, technology, and capital resources allocation with strategic initiatives;
- Past performance in offering new products or services and evaluating potential and consummated acquisitions;
- Performance in implementing new technology or systems;
- The effectiveness of management's methods of communicating, implementing, and modifying strategic plans, and consistency with stated risk tolerance;
- The adequacy and independence of controls to monitor business decisions;
- The responsiveness to identified deficiencies in internal controls; and
- The quality, integrity, timeliness, and relevance of reports that the board of directors must have to oversee strategic decisions.

4.   Reach a conclusion on aggregate strategic risk from personal fiduciary services.

Reputation Risk

Conclusion: Aggregate reputation risk from personal fiduciary services is (low, moderate, high).

Objective: To identify and estimate reputation risk from the bank's delivery and administration of personal fiduciary services.

1. Discuss with management the impact of the strategic factors listed below on reputation risk from personal fiduciary services:

    -   The volume and types of assets and number of accounts under management or administration;
    -   Merger and acquisition plans and opportunities;
    -   Multi-state fiduciary operations; and
    -   Potential or planned entrance into new businesses, product lines, or technologies (including new delivery channels), particularly those that may test legal boundaries.

2. Discuss with management the impact of the external factors listed below on reputation risk from personal fiduciary services:

    -   The market or public's perception of the corporate mission, culture, and risk tolerance of the bank;
    -   The market or public's perception of the bank's financial stability;
    -   The market or public's perception of the quality of products and services offered by the bank; and
    -   The impact of economic, industry, and market conditions; legislative and regulatory change; technological advances; and competition.

3. Obtain and analyze conclusions from the personal fiduciary services "Quality of Risk Management" examination procedures. Incorporate those conclusions into the evaluation of reputation risk from personal fiduciary services. Consider the following factors:

- Past performance in offering new products or services and in conducting due diligence prior to startup;
- Past performance in developing or implementing new technologies and systems;
- The nature and amount of litigation and customer complaints;
- The expertise of senior management and the effectiveness of the board of directors in maintaining an ethical, self-policing culture;
- Management's willingness and ability to adjust strategies based on regulatory changes, market disruptions, market or public perception, and litigation losses;
- The quality and integrity of management information systems and the development of expanded or newly integrated systems;
- The adequacy and independence of internal control;
- The responsiveness to deficiencies in internal control;
- The ability to minimize exposure from litigation and customer complaints;
- The ability to communicate effectively with the market, public, and media;
- Policies, practices, and systems protecting information customers might consider private or confidential from deliberate or accidental disclosure; and
- Management's responsiveness to internal, external, and regulatory review findings.

4. Reach a conclusion on aggregate reputation risk from personal fiduciary services.

Personal Fiduciary Services Quality of Risk Management

Conclusion: The quality of risk management for personal fiduciary services is (strong, satisfactory, weak).

Policies

Conclusion: The board has adopted (strong, satisfactory, weak) personal fiduciary services policies.

Objective: To determine the quality of established policies and procedures and their consistency with the bank's fiduciary strategic direction.

1. Identify and obtain the bank's policies and strategic plan relating to personal fiduciary services.

2. Evaluate the policy and procedures. Consider the following:

   - Is the policy formally approved and periodically reviewed by the board or a designated committee?

   - Does the policy adequately address applicable law including 12 Part CFR 9.5?

   - Does the policy establish a risk management and internal control framework that addresses the following?

     - Organizational and functional charts;
     - Defined lines of authority and responsibility;
     - Delegation authority and approval processes;
     - Processes to select, employ, and evaluate legal counsel;
     - Standards for dealings with affiliated organizations; and
     - Personnel practices.

   - Does the policy include appropriate account acceptance and administration guidelines that address

- New account acceptance processes,
- Account reviews,
- Discretionary distributions,
- Investment reviews,
- Cash management,
- Bank Secrecy Act compliance and anti-money laundering controls,
- Customer information privacy,
- Fees and other expenses,
- Tax preparation and reporting, and
- Account closings.

- Does the policy effectively address information systems and technology applications? Consider

  - Accounting and other transaction record keeping systems,
  - Management information system requirements,
  - Customer information security, and
  - Systems security and disaster contingency plans.

- Does the policy establish

  - Policy exception definitions and guidelines,
  - Policy exception tracking and reporting processes,
  - Client reporting guidelines,
  - Control self-assessment processes, and
  - Customer complaint resolution procedures?

Are these guidelines and processes adequate?

3. Review the strategic plan and supporting financial projections and determine whether the policy is consistent with the bank's strategic goals and objectives.

4. Review how strategic initiatives and policies are communicated within the organization and determine whether the communication processes are adequate.

5.   If deficiencies are identified in the policymaking and implementation process, discuss them with management and document the conclusions and recommendations.

6.   Finalize and document conclusions on the quality and consistency of the bank's fiduciary policy and procedures.

Processes

Conclusion: Management has adopted (strong, satisfactory, weak) processes for personal fiduciary services.

Objective: To determine the quality and effectiveness of account acceptance processes.

1.   Evaluate the bank's account acceptance process.

- Is the process formalized and adequately documented?
- Is appropriate information obtained during the due diligence review and effectively used in the approval process?
- Is the process complied with? Does it include an appropriate approval process for policy exceptions?
- Does the acceptance process comply with 12 CFR Part 9.6(a), Pre-acceptance Reviews?

2.   Select a sample of recently accepted personal fiduciary accounts for review. If possible, include a variety of account types including successor trustee and co-trustee accounts.

3.   For each selected account, determine whether the account acceptance process was effective and adequately considered

- The bank's level of technical expertise and operational capabilities;
- The bank's proposed fiduciary duties and obligations and the limits of each party's status as agent or fiduciary;

- The terms and conditions of the governing instrument and the character of the account parties;
- Current or foreseeable problems in administering the account;
- The adequacy of compensation for accepting the risks from administering the account;
- The types of assets currently in the portfolio and the types of assets to be purchased and managed in the portfolio;
- Environmental review issues;
- Input from portfolio managers, risk managers, and legal counsel;
- Potential or actual conflicts of interests;
- Prior fiduciary administration particularly successor trustee accounts; and
- Co-trustee relationships.

4. For selected successor trustee accounts, evaluate the bank's review of prior fiduciary administration of the trusts.

    - If there was a previous trustee, has that trustee properly resigned or been removed in a legally acceptable manner?

    - Does the trust document or state law provide the bank with protection from acts of the predecessor trustee? Consider the use of waivers and exculpatory language in the governing instrument. If not, has the bank determined whether

        - The prior fiduciary has fully accounted for its actions,

        - The prior fiduciary has accounted to the correct parties and been fully released, and

        - Such release extends to the successor trustee?

    - Did the bank obtain prior fiduciary tax records and review them for consistency with current statements, accountings, and asset inventories? If discrepancies were identified, did the bank take appropriate action?

5.   Evaluate the adequacy and effectiveness of the following:

- Checklists or other methods used to ensure that all the necessary documentation is obtained for the account. Are original or authenticated copies of the governing instrument obtained and adequately secured, including court orders and inventories?

- Receipts, inventories, and appraisals for court-supervised accounts, or schedules of assets delivered to the bank or the bank's control for custody and protection.

- Administrative files that contain

  - Synoptic data which should summarize the governing instrument provisions, including investment and retention powers, income remittances, dispositive provisions, corpus invasions, and other important authorizations (records of names of parties-in-interest, co-fiduciaries, and other relevant historical data should be part of this information);
  - Legal documents;
  - Correspondence;
  - Account reviews;
  - Investment transactions;
  - Tax documents and reports; and
  - Regulatory filings.

- Tickler files or other tracking methods relating to the preparation and timely execution of future duties such as account reviews, income remittances, principal distributions, insurance and tax deadlines, fee and statement information and termination events.

6.   Evaluate the initial post-acceptance review for each selected account. Determine whether the review includes

- A review of the governing instrument and a determination of its purpose, intent, investment guidelines and powers;

- A review of all discretionary assets to determine whether they are appropriate for the account as required by 12 CFR Part 9.6(b);

- A determination of compliance with internal policies and procedures; and

- Approval of an appropriate investment policy statement.

Objective: To determine the quality of account administration processes.

1. Select an appropriate sample of established fiduciary accounts. A sufficient number of accounts should be selected to form a reliable assessment of the bank's processes. Account selection may be based on risk factors such as size, complexity, litigation, and insider relationships, but the sample must be of sufficient size to satisfy the examination's objectives.

2. Review each selected account and determine whether administrative processes are adequate and effective. Determine whether

- The account's activity complies with the terms of the governing instrument and meets the needs of account beneficiaries according to their circumstances;
- The account's activity complies with federal, state and local laws, and court orders and directions;
- The bank performs account reviews in accordance with 12 CFR Part 9.6(c) and other applicable law;
- The bank prepares and provides accurate account statements and required court accountings;
- The bank avoids conflicts of interest and self-dealing;

- The bank charges and reports accurate account fees and complies with compensation provisions of 12 CFR Part 9.15; and
- Any services provided a third-party vendor are properly performed and the vendor's charges are appropriate and reasonable.

3. Determine whether fiduciary managers and administrators have an adequate knowledge and understanding of the accounts assigned to them:

- Are fiduciary accounts assigned to a specific administrator?

- Are fiduciary managers aware of account problems such as litigation, complaints, and other important administrative matters?

- Have account administrators maintained account files in accordance with policy and sound administrative practices?

4. Evaluate the bank's processes for administering co-trustee accounts:

- Determine whether proper and timely written authorizations are obtained from co-fiduciaries or others whose approval may be required for important actions;

- Determine the effectiveness of the process of obtaining and following up on co-fiduciary and grantor approvals.

5. Evaluate the bank's account cash management processes:

- Identify and review large uninvested or undistributed cash balances and discuss them with management. Determine whether administration of the particular accounts is appropriate and complies with 12 CFR Part 9.10, Fiduciary funds awaiting investment or distribution.

- Review account overdrafts, giving attention to large and longstanding items. Determine why they exist and discuss management's plans to clear them.

6. Evaluate the bank's discretionary distribution processes:

    - Is the decision-making authority for discretionary distributions expressly defined and communicated to all personnel?

    - Are decisions fully documented and authorized by designated personnel or committees?

    - Are distributions consistent with the guidelines established in the governing instrument? Consider the following:

        - Language in the governing instrument.
        - Intent of the grantor.
        - Need for the payment and the purpose for which it will be used.
        - Needs of other beneficiaries.
        - Size and duration of the fiduciary account.
        - Number, ages, and standard of living of the beneficiaries.
        - Other assets or sources of income available to the beneficiary.
        - Tax consequences of a distribution.

7. Evaluate the bank's record keeping and client reporting processes:

    - Is account income properly received and recorded? Does the bank properly allocate cash to income and principal in accordance with the governing instrument or state law?

    - Do disbursements and expenditures comply with the governing instrument, other applicable law, and internal policy?

- Are account fees and other charges appropriate, accurate, and consistent with applicable law?

- Does the bank have an account statement distribution policy and supporting procedures? Is the bank complying with the policy?

- Are statements prepared and distributed to persons entitled to them?

8. Review fiduciary tax administration and evaluate the process to prepare and file fiduciary related tax returns:

- Is the amount of estimated quarterly taxes paid to the IRS adequately supported?
- Are estate taxes (federal and state) paid within the time limits required by the IRS?
- Are federal and state tax returns filed on time?
- Are fair evaluations performed on estate assets?
- Are the effects of the generation-skipping tax considered on distributions to younger generations?

9. Evaluate the bank's process for closing fiduciary accounts:

- Is the process clearly defined with specified approval authority?
- Is a review by legal counsel part of the process?
- Are appropriate allocations of income determined at the time of closing?
- Is the fee unit notified when an account is terminated?
- Are estate and federal income tax issues appropriately considered?
- Is an adequate plan of distribution created?
- Are judicial accountings appropriately administered?

Objective: To determine the adequacy and effectiveness of internal control within the personal fiduciary organization.

1. As appropriate and approved by the bank EIC and internal

control examiner, select and complete appropriate internal control examination procedures from the "Internal Control" booklet of the *Comptroller's Handbook*.

2. After completing the examination procedures selected above and reviewing the results of the control systems examination procedures, draw conclusions on internal control for personal fiduciary services.

	Strong	Satisfactory	Weak
Control Environment			
Risk Assessment			
Control Activities			
Accounting, Information, and Communication			
Self-assessment and Monitoring			

The overall system of internal control for personal fiduciary services is

	Strong	Satisfactory	Weak

3. Submit the assessment of internal control to the examiner responsible for evaluating internal control for asset management activities.

Objective: To determine the adequacy and effectiveness of third-party vendor selection and monitoring processes.

1. Review policies and procedures for the selection and monitoring of third-party vendors. Discuss the process with management and document significant weaknesses in risk management processes. Consider the following:

   - The quality of the due diligence review process;
   - The contract negotiation and approval process;
   - Risk assessment processes;

- Risk management and audit division participation;
- Vendor monitoring processes, such as the assignment of responsibility, the frequency of reviews, and the quality of information reports reviewed; and
- Vendor problem resolution process.

2. Obtain a list of vendors used by the bank to provide fiduciary services and support. Select a sample from the vendor list and evaluate the adequacy and effectiveness of the bank's selection and monitoring processes for each vendor selected.

Objective: Determine the adequacy and effectiveness of processes used to develop and approve new products, services, or lines of business.

1. Evaluate how management plans for and develops new products and services. Consider the following:

- Types of market research conducted, such as product feasibility studies;
- Cost, pricing, and profitability analyses;
- Risk assessment processes;
- Legal counsel and review;
- Role of risk management and audit functions;
- Information systems and technology impact; and
- Human resource requirements.

2. Evaluate the product approval process by selecting a sample of products or services developed and rolled out since the last examination of this area:

- Is the approval authority clearly established and adhered to?
- Were bank policies and procedures adequately followed?
- Does the process require adequate documentation of the factors considered and adequate support for the final decision?

Personnel

Conclusion: The bank has (strong, satisfactory, weak) personnel for personal fiduciary services.

Objective: To determine the quality of fiduciary management and supporting personnel.

1. Obtain a list of fiduciary management and key supporting personnel that includes the following information:

    - Title and job responsibilities,
    - Formal education and training, and
    - Related work experience and accomplishments.

    Fiduciary management will include any bank director, fiduciary committee member, fiduciary manager, account administrator, third-party vendor, or other bank employee responsible for developing, approving, or implementing fiduciary business strategies, policies, and information systems.

2. Review fiduciary management and supporting personnel and determine whether management is

    - Competent based on the complexity of the bank's personal fiduciary lines of business;

    - Knowledgeable of fiduciary policies, strategic plans, and risk tolerance standards; and

    - Aware of the bank's code of ethics, if applicable, and committed to high ethical standards.

3. Evaluate the adequacy of staffing levels by reviewing and discussing

    - Current strategic initiatives and financial goals;
    - Current business volume, complexity, and risk profile;
    - Recent staffing analyses and recommendations; and

- The impact of company cost-cutting programs, if applicable.

4. Compare job descriptions and other responsibilities of managers and key supporting personnel with their experience, education, and other training.

   - Are personnel qualified and adequately trained for positions and responsibilities?

   - Does the number of clients or accounts assigned to administrators appear reasonable?

   - Are personnel performing tasks outside their job descriptions that adversely affect their overall performance or risk levels?

Objective: To determine the adequacy and effectiveness of the bank's personnel policies, practices, and programs.

1. Determine whether lines of authority and individual duties and responsibilities are clearly defined and communicated.

2. Evaluate the bank's recruitment and employee retention program by reviewing the following:

   - Recent success in hiring and retaining high-quality personnel;
   - Level and trends of staff turnover, particularly in key positions; and
   - The quality and reasonableness of management succession plans.

3. Analyze the bank's compensation and performance evaluation program:

   - Is the program formalized and periodically reviewed by the board and senior management?

- Is the program consistent with the bank's risk tolerance and ethical standards?

- Are responsibilities and accountability standards clearly established for the performance evaluation program?

- Is the program applied consistently and functioning as intended?

- Does the program reward behavior and performance that is consistent with the bank's ethical culture, risk tolerance standards, and strategic initiatives?

- Does the program include an adequate mechanism for the board to evaluate management performance?

4. Review the training program by considering the following:

- The types and frequency of training and whether the program is adequate and effective;

- How much of the fiduciary budget is allocated to training and whether the financial resources applied are adequate; and

- Whether employee training needs and accomplishments are a component of the performance evaluation program.

Control Systems

Conclusion: The bank has (strong, satisfactory, weak) control systems for personal fiduciary services.

Objective: To determine the quality of board and management risk controls and monitoring systems.

1. Determine and evaluate the types of fiduciary risk control and monitoring systems used by the board and management.

Consider the following:

- Board and senior management fiduciary information reports;
- Fiduciary risk management groups;
- Fiduciary committee structures, responsibilities, and performance;
- Management information systems;
- Compliance programs;
- Control self-assessments; and
- Audit program.

2. Determine the extent to which the board and senior management are involved in fiduciary risk control and monitoring. Consider:

- The types and frequency of board and senior management fiduciary reviews used to determine adherence to policies, operating procedures, and strategic initiatives;

- The accuracy, timeliness, relevance, and distribution of management information reports;

- The responsiveness to risk control deficiencies and the effectiveness of corrective action and follow-up activities;

- The frequency, content, and usefulness of litigation reports; and

- The responsiveness to internal and external audits and regulatory examinations.

3. If applicable, evaluate the compliance program. Consider:

- The strength of board and senior management commitment and support;
- Line management responsibility and accountability;
- Program formalization, transaction testing, reporting structures, and follow-up processes;

- Qualifications and performance of compliance officer and supporting personnel;
- Communication systems; and
- Training programs.

4. If the bank has implemented a control self-assessment program, obtain information on its assessment of controls in the personal fiduciary services area. Evaluate the program and the results of recent control self-assessments of business and support functions.

5. Review the bank's audit activity relating to personal fiduciary services. A key goal of this review is to determine how reliable the internal and external audit work is. In the course of the review,

    - Select and complete appropriate examination procedures from the "Internal and External Audits" booklet of the *Comptroller's Handbook*. Coordinate the selection of procedures with the examiner responsible for evaluating the bank's audit program.

    - Obtain appropriate internal audit reports, work papers, and follow-up reports. Disseminate the reports to the appropriate examiners for review and follow-up.

    - Determine the adequacy and effectiveness of the internal audit program by reviewing

        - The timing, scope, and results of audit activity;
        - The quality of audit reports, work papers and follow-up processes; and
        - The independence, qualifications and competency of audit staff.

    - If the review of audit reports and work papers raises questions about audit effectiveness, discuss the issues with appropriate examiners and determine whether the scope of the audit review should be expanded. Issues that might require an expanded scope include

- Unexplained or unexpected changes in auditors or significant changes in the audit program;
- Inadequate scope of the audit program;
- Audit work papers that are deficient or do not support audit conclusions;
- High-growth areas without adequate audit coverage; and
- Inappropriate actions by insiders to influence the findings or scope of audits.

6. Draw conclusions about the adequacy and effectiveness of the audit program and forward the findings and recommendations, if applicable, to the examiner responsible for evaluating the bank's audit program.

Personal Fiduciary Services Examination Conclusions

Objective: To consolidate the conclusions and recommendations from the personal fiduciary examination activities into final conclusions on the quantity of risk and quality of risk management.

1. Obtain conclusion memoranda and other risk assessment products from completed examination procedures.

2. Discuss the individual examination findings with the responsible examiners and ensure that conclusions and recommendations are accurate, supported, and appropriately communicated.

3. Determine and document the recommended rating for the "compliance" element based on the factors listed in the Uniform Interagency Trust Rating System (UITRS).

4. Finalize quantity of risk and quality of risk management conclusions for input into the following, where applicable:

   - Core knowledge database
   - Core assessment standards (CAS)
   - Risk assessment system (RAS)
   - Uniform Interagency Trust Rating System (UITRS)
   - CAMELS
   - Report of examination
   - Asset management profile (AMP)

Objective: To communicate examination findings and initiate corrective action, if applicable.

1. Provide the EIC the following information, when applicable:

   - Examination summary comments for the core assessment.
   - Comments applicable to the RAS.
   - UITRS ratings recommendations.
   - Draft report of examination comments.
   - Matters requiring attention (MRA).
   - Violations of law and regulation and corrective action.

- Other recommendations provided to bank management.

2. Discuss examination findings with the EIC and adjust findings and recommendations as needed. If the UITRS compliance rating is 3 or worse, or the level of any risk factor is moderate and increasing or high because of the impact of personal fiduciary activities, contact the supervisory office before conducting the exit meeting with management.

3. Hold an exit meeting with appropriate fiduciary committees and/or other risk managers to communicate examination conclusions and obtain commitments for corrective action, if applicable. Allow management time before the meeting to review draft examination conclusions and report comments.

4. Prepare final comments for the report of examination as requested by the EIC. Perform a final check to determine whether comments

   - Meet OCC report of examination guidelines.
   - Support assigned UITRS ratings.
   - Contain accurate violation citations.

5. If there are MRA comments, enter them in the OCC's electronic information system. Ensure that the comments are consistent with MRA content requirements.

6. Prepare appropriate comments for the fiduciary examination conclusion memorandum. Supplement the memorandum's comments, when appropriate, to include the following:

   - The objectives and scope of completed supervisory activities;
   - Reasons for changes in the supervisory strategy, if applicable;
   - Overall conclusions, recommendations for corrective action, and management commitments and time frames; and

- Comments on any recommended administrative actions, enforcement actions, and civil money penalty referrals.

7. Update applicable sections of the OCC's electronic information system.

8. Prepare an updated supervisory strategy for personal fiduciary services and provide it to the asset management EIC for review and approval.

9. Prepare a memorandum or update work programs with any information that will facilitate future examinations.

10. Organize and reference work papers in accordance with OCC guidelines.

11. Complete and distribute assignment evaluations for assisting examiners.

Appendix A: Types of Personal Trusts

This section provides general information on various types of personal trusts. Bank fiduciaries should consult with appropriate legal and tax counsel for comprehensive guidance on the proper use and ramifications of these types of trust instruments.

Grantor Trusts

A grantor is a person who transfers property by deed or who grants property rights by means of a trust instrument or some other document. A grantor trust is a living trust in which the grantor, because of certain rights to income or principal or certain power over the disposition of income and principal, is treated as the owner of the trust and taxed on the income thereof. A grantor trust is not treated as a separate entity for income tax purposes.

A grantor trust may be revocable or irrevocable depending on the planning needs of the grantor. This type of trust provides many lifetime advantages to the grantor. The grantor retains control over the trust's assets during his or her lifetime. In addition, assets owned by the trust will be held or distributed at the death of the grantor in accordance with the trust agreement and will not be subject to probate administration.

Declaration of Trust

A basic grantor trust used when the grantor wants to have the trust operational and have full control. The grantor declares himself to be trustee of certain identified assets and serves as the initial trustee.

Grantor Retained Annuity Trust (GRAT)

A GRAT is an irrevocable trust in which the grantor retains the right to a set annual dollar amount (the annuity) for a fixed term and gives the principal to others, such as the grantor's children, at the end of that term. If the grantor survives until the end of the annuity term, all of the trust principal will be excluded from the grantor's estate for estate tax purposes.

Since this is a lifetime transfer into an irrevocable trust, the gift must be valued for gift tax purposes using IRS rules. The favorable tax consequences on the value of the gift allow the grantor and the beneficiaries to benefit from any increase in the value of the gift without paying estate taxes.

Grantor Retained Income Trust (GRIT)

In a GRIT, the grantor retains the right to receive all of the trust's income for a fixed term and gives the principal to others, such as the grantor's children, at the end of that term. If the grantor survives until the end of the income term, all principal will be excluded from the grantor's estate for tax purposes. In most cases, a transfer to a GRIT will be treated as an outright gift to the remaindermen.

Grantor Retained Unitrust Trust (GRUT)

A GRUT is identical to a GRAT in every way except that the income interest retained by the grantor is a unitrust interest. That is, each year the trustee calculates the amount of the interest payment as a percentage of the market value of the trust property. This type of trust is particularly useful if the grantor intends to add assets to the trust.

Standby Trusts

A standby trust, or "pour over" trust, is so-named because one of its purposes is to receive the grantor's assets upon his death. Some jurisdictions require that these trusts be funded with a nominal amount of trust property in order to be effective; others do not. By creating one of these trusts, assets owned by the grantor at death can "pour over" into the trust. This trust has two major benefits:

1.   Funds can be quickly transferred to the trust, if necessary.

2.   Property may also be transferred to the trust under the residuary clause of the testator's will. The grantor obtains

---

additional privacy because terms of a standby trust are not made public, unlike the terms of a testamentary trust.

Crummey Trusts

Beneficiaries of a trust with "crummey powers" are granted a limited power to withdraw property that is earned or contributed to the trust. This power is set for a limited amount of time in the trust agreement. Giving the beneficiary the right to immediate possession allows transfers to the trust to qualify for the annual gift tax exclusion. The power is generally limited to the amount excludable from gift tax liability under the annual gift tax exclusion or the greater of $5,000 or 5 percent of the trust property. It is an especially useful way to make gifts to minors since distribution of the trust corpus is not required when the minor attains age 21.

In order to take advantage of the federal gift tax exclusion, a donor must make a gift of a present interest to the trust. The beneficiaries must be provided the power to withdraw the contributed property outright. If the beneficiaries decline to withdraw the contributed property from the trust, the property is available to satisfy the primary purpose of the trust. The IRS requires that beneficiaries receive actual, timely notice of their rights prior to the lapse of such rights. While this strategy may be used to accumulate annual gifts using any investment device, insurance contracts historically have been the most prevalent and provide the most certainty.

Life Insurance Trusts

Life insurance trusts or "wealth replacement trusts" are used for estate planning, business continuation, liquidity needs, or other considerations of the customer. Life insurance proceeds are generally subject to estate tax in the estate of the owner of the policy.

Revocable Life Insurance Trusts. Like a standby trust, a revocable insurance trust is funded with a nominal amount of trust property during the settlor's lifetime. The trust is designated as the recipient of life insurance proceeds upon the settlor's death, and the trust becomes fully funded with the insurance proceeds. This arrangement is used when the settlor does not have significant assets to be managed during his or her lifetime, but has significant insurance benefits that should be managed upon death.

Irrevocable Life Insurance Trusts. Life insurance can be purchased by, or assigned to, an irrevocable trust to shelter insurance proceeds from the estate tax that would be imposed if the owner of the policy died while owning it. The life insurance policy is usually the sole asset of the trust while the insured is alive. The trust is generally the beneficiary of the insurance policy and holds title to the insurance policy during the life of the insured. The settlor is allowed to make gifts of present interest to the trust for the purpose of purchasing life insurance. The settlor may either pay the premiums for the policy or forward the money to the trustee for payment of the premiums. The trust usually includes "crummey powers" giving trust beneficiaries current withdrawal rights over amounts transferred to the trust so that these transfers will qualify for the annual gift tax exclusion.

Upon the death of the insured, the trustee will follow the terms of the trust concerning the use of the insurance policy proceeds. Some insurance trusts are funded with other assets for the trustee to manage and to use those assets to pay the life insurance policy premiums.

One of the trustee's responsibilities is to ensure that the trust's tax benefits are preserved. The bank should have controls to ensure that the following requirements are met:

- The trust agreement must include "crummey powers." The trustee must inform the beneficiaries of their right to withdraw principal from the trust. Documentation must be maintained as evidence that these notices have been sent to all beneficiaries.

- The insured must not hold at death, and must not have held in the previous three years, any incident of ownership in the insurance policy. The trustee must have total control of the policy if the proceeds are to be withheld from the insured's estate.

- The proceeds of the life insurance policy may not be paid to the estate of the insured, nor can they be used in a manner that directly benefits the estate. Although the trust is intended to benefit the estate indirectly, the trustee cannot be under any obligation to pay the insured's estate taxes. If such payments are made, the entire amount of the insurance proceeds must be included in the insured's estate.

Marital Deduction Trusts

Marital deduction trusts are used to transfer a decedent's property into trust and take advantage of the unlimited marital deduction. Transfers of property to a marital deduction trust are designed to be exempt from federal gift or estate tax. Many states provide the same deductions. The settlor may choose among several types of marital deduction trusts.

General Power of Appointment (GPA)

A marital deduction trust with a GPA gives the surviving spouse beneficiary maximum control of the trust property during his or her life. The spouse may withdraw part or all of the trust property and may exercise a general power of appointment over the trust property during life and/or at death. Trust assets are subject to estate tax on the spouse's death.

Qualified Terminable Interest Property Trust (QTIP)

A QTIP trust is used to provide a surviving spouse financial support and retain control over the distribution of the trust's assets when the lifetime beneficiary spouse dies. A QTIP trust allows a settlor to ensure that his or her assets will ultimately pass to chosen beneficiaries. The executor may be given power to elect none, some, or all of the trust property for the marital deduction. The executor makes the QTIP election when the first spouse dies.

In order to qualify for the unlimited marital deduction, the trustee must ensure that the following criteria are met:

- All net accounting income must be paid at least annually to the spouse.

- No person, including the spouse, may have the right to appoint the property to anyone other than the spouse during the spouse's life.

Estate Trusts

An estate trust pays income to a surviving spouse or accumulates all of its income. Upon the surviving spouse's death, trust assets must be distributed to the surviving spouse's probate estate. Estate trusts are rarely used marital deduction trusts, but do qualify for the marital deduction and are treated as a separate taxpayer for income tax purposes.

Qualified Domestic Trust

Qualified domestic trusts are federal marital deduction trusts for the benefit of spouses who are not U.S. citizens. The purpose of this trust is to qualify assets left to a nonresident, non-citizen spouse for the marital deduction. This type of trust is similar to a QTIP, but has additional restrictions.

Credit Shelter Trust

A credit shelter trust (also called a bypass or family trust) is designed to take advantage of a U.S. taxpayer's unified credit against the U.S. gift or estate tax. Many states have similar credits. Typically, an individual creates a credit shelter trust in the amount of the unified credit established in the tax code, and property placed in the trust is not included in the decedent's estate for tax purposes. The decedent's surviving spouse is typically the trust income beneficiary, and the trust will normally terminate on the death of the surviving spouse. Remaining trust property passes to the remainderman free of estate tax.

This trust is usually designed to pass family wealth to the settlor's descendents while making the property available to the surviving spouse during his or her lifetime. Both income and principal may be distributed to the spouse or other individuals during the term of the trust. Credit shelter trusts can be created during the settlor's lifetime, although it is more typically created by will as part of a testamentary estate plan.

Generation-Skipping Trust (GST)

The generation-skipping transfer tax (GSTT) is a flat tax on any transfer to a grandchild or more remote descendant. Each U.S. taxpayer has a specific dollar exemption from this tax. A GST takes advantage of this exemption by transferring property up to the exemption amount to a trust for the benefit of trust beneficiaries who are two or more generations beyond or below the settlor. If structured properly, the trust property can pass to the future generations without payment of the transfer tax. A settlor may have reasons other than avoiding the transfer tax for establishing the trust.

A GST typically benefits the settlor's grandchildren, who may be present, future, or contingent beneficiaries. For example, a GST may be established to benefit the settlor's children and grandchildren during their lifetimes, with trust property distributing outright to grandchildren on the children's death. Alternatively, a GST may continue for the longest term allowed by state law, most of which are governed by the rule against perpetuities. The settlor may allocate his or her generation-skipping tax exemption to the amounts contributed to the trust. The tax goal of the GST is to avoid estate tax at the death of the settlor's children.

Even with the enactment of the Economic Growth and Tax Relief Reconciliation Act of 2001, and its temporary repeal of estate taxes until 2011, settlors continue to seek to avoid both quantifiable as well as potential future estate taxes. In order to close a loophole in the estate tax provisions, the tax code imposes the GSTT. The GSTT is intended to capture transfers made by a donor to beneficiaries two or more generations above or below the donor ("skip persons") such as a grandchild. An exemption to the GSTT allows approximately $1 million to pass untaxed from a donor to skip-generation individuals.

Dynasty trusts are commonly created to utilize the settlor's and the settlor's spouse's GSTT exemptions. Dynasty trusts are specialized irrevocable trusts designed to shelter assets from transfer taxes over multiple generations of the settlor's family. By virtue of the extensive term of the trust, the trust property and its future appreciation can be sheltered from estate taxation beyond multiple deaths in a family.

Minor Exclusion Trust (2503(c) Trust)

A minor exclusion trust is established for the benefit of a minor and attempts to qualify for the annual gift tax exclusion of the settlor. The trust can be made to last until the minor reaches the age of 21. The trust must provide that its principal and income can be used for the benefit of the minor beneficiary before he or she attains 21 years of age. Any property remaining in the trust must be transferred to the beneficiary when the beneficiary attains age 21. The trust can be structured so that it continues after the beneficiary reaches 21 if the beneficiary has the right to demand a distribution at 21.

The establishment of a 2503(c) trust creates a separate taxable entity for both income and estate tax purposes. As a trust, it differs from the agency arrangements established under the Uniform Gift to Minors Act or the Uniform Transfers to Minors Act and is designed to ensure separation of the trust assets from the grantor's taxable estate.

Charitable Trusts

A charitable trust is a trust created for the benefit of a legal charity. There are two types of charitable trusts: charitable remainder and charitable lead trusts.

Charitable Remainder Trusts (CRTs)

CRTs are irrevocable trusts established for the life of the donor or other non-charitable life beneficiaries with the remainder payable to a charity at the death of the life beneficiaries. CRTs may be either inter vivos or testamentary trusts. The grantor may choose to retain the income from the CRT over his or her lifetime, or the grantor may divert the income to another beneficiary.

A CRT is also called a split interest trust because the income interest and remainder interest go to different parties. This type of trust has two purposes: First, it pays any income or annuity interest earned by the trust assets to the income beneficiaries. Second, it transfers the trust's assets to a charity upon the death of the beneficiaries or at the end of the trust term. While the income payout period for this arrangement may generally not exceed 20 years, a term based on the life expectancy of the income beneficiaries may exceed the 20-year limit.

This type of trust is very attractive to people whose assets have a low cost basis and produce little income. (For example, real estate holdings or securities owned for many years.) A CRT allows the donor to realize an immediate income tax deduction. The deduction is computed using IRS actuarial tables to determine the value of the remainder interest going to the charity. The older the donor, the greater the deduction. The donor also avoids what may be substantial capital gains taxes on the sale of the donated property by the trustee. The governing instrument must be specific to ensure that the charitable deduction is realized. Two types of CRT differ in how they calculate payments to beneficiaries:

- **Charitable remainder annuity trust.** This arrangement pays the annuity beneficiary a fixed annual amount during his or her lifetime. That annual amount must be at least 5 percent of the value of the property when the trust was established. The remainder interest goes to the qualified charity at the annuitant's death.

- **Charitable remainder unitrust.** This arrangement provides that the lifetime income beneficiary will receive a fixed percentage (at least 5 percent) of the fair market value of the trust calculated annually. The remainder interest must be given to a qualified charity.

Charitable Lead Trust (CLT)

CLTs are the reverse of CRTs because they allow a grantor to provide the interest income from the trust to a qualified charity for a defined period of time with the remaining assets reverting back to the grantor or to named beneficiaries at the end of the trust's term. A charitable lead trust can be either inter vivos or testamentary.

This type of trust is attractive for a donor who regularly makes gifts to charity. Using this type of arrangement, the donor can continue to make the charitable contributions while retaining the remainder interest in the property for the benefit of the heirs. The value of the taxable gift can be substantially reduced, thereby eliminating the taxes paid during the donor's lifetime. Like the remainder trust, the lead trust can be an annuity trust or a unitrust.

Pre-need Funeral Trusts

These trusts are generally marketed by the funeral industry and are designed to pay the funeral expenses of the grantor, including the casket, gravestone, funeral plot and perpetual care. The laws and regulations governing these trusts vary from state to state. Although many states require banks to serve as trustees of these trusts, some allow funeral directors or other parties to serve as trustee. Depending upon state law and contract terms, a pre-need funeral trust may be revocable or irrevocable. Usually, the consumer has the choice. An irrevocable trust may be necessary to enable consumers to maintain their eligibility for state or federal income assistance. An OCC memorandum dated April 11, 2000 provides additional information concerning risks associated with pre-need funeral trusts.

Appendix B: Uniform Trust Laws

"Model" or "uniform" acts are promulgated by legal and trade groups to standardize state laws. State legislatures may adopt these model laws as drafted or modify them to meet the needs of their particular states. Examples of uniform laws include the following:

Uniform Trust Act of 1999
Uniform Probate Code
Uniform Trustees' Powers Act
Uniform Fiduciaries Act
Uniform Prudent Investor Act (1994)
Revised Uniform Principal and Income Act (1997)
Uniform Custodial Trust Act
Uniform Gifts to Minors Act
Uniform Transfers to Minors Act
Uniform Supervision of Trustees for Charitable Purposes
Uniform Act for Simplification of Fiduciary Security Transfers
Uniform Testamentary Additions to Trusts Act (1991)
Uniform Statutory Rule Against Perpetuities Act

References

Laws

12 USC 92a

The Gramm-Leach-Bliley Act of 1999 amending the Securities and Exchange Act of 1934

Uniting and Strengthening America by Providing Appropriate Tools Required to Intercept and Obstruct Terrorism Act of 2001

Internal Revenue Code, Publications, and Interpretations

Economic Growth and Tax Relief Reconciliation Act of 2001 amending the Internal Revenue Code

Regulations

12 CFR 9, Fiduciary Activities of National Banks

OCC Issuances

OCC Bulletin 97-22, "Fiduciary Activities of National Banks, Qs and As — 12 CFR Part 9"

OCC Bulletin 98-46, "Uniform Interagency Trust Rating System"

OCC Bulletin 2001-26, "Privacy of Consumer Financial Information"

OCC Bulletin 2001-47, "Third-Party Relationships"

OCC Memorandum: "Pre-need Funeral Trust Accounts," April 11, 2000

Comptroller's Handbook Booklets

"Large Bank Supervision"

"Community Bank Supervision"

"Asset Management"

"Community Bank Fiduciary Activities Supervision"

"Conflicts of Interest"

"Investment Management Services"

"Consumer Compliance"

"Bank Secrecy Act/Anti-money Laundering"

"Insurance Activities"

Treatises

Restatement of the Law, Trusts, 2nd and 3rd, American Law Institute

The Law of Trusts, 4th Edition, Austin W. Scott and William F. Fratcher

Case Law

Crummey v. Commissioner of the I.R.S., 397 F.2d 82 (9th Cir. 1968)

Other Reference Sources

Fiduciary Law and Trust Activities Guide, 2000, American Bankers Association

Building Trust Expertise, Trust Administration, Taxation, and Asset Management, 1999, American Bankers Association